Management Dynamics of the 21st Century

Management Dynamics of the 21st Century

Soumak Palit

KALPAZ

First Published, 2017

Published by

Kalpaz Publications
C-30, Satyawati Nagar,
Delhi – 110052
E-mail: kalpaz@hotmail.com
Ph.: 9212142040

Printed at: G. Print Process, Delhi

Cataloging in Publication Data—DK

Courtesy: D.K. Agencies (P) Ltd. <docinfo@dkagencies.com>

Palit, Soumak, author.

Management dynamics of the 21st century / Soumak Palit.
pages cm
ISBN 9789351283492 (hardback)

1. Management—India. 2. Economic development—India. I. Title.

HD70.I4P35 2017 DDC 658.400954 23

Contents

Foreword

This is a very interesting book for students, teachers, trainers, managers, entrepreneurs and even politicians. It deals with the fundamentals of ***Arthashastra***- "the science of benefit, of practical life"; and economics is indeed unsentimental and practical. Therefore this book appeals to me as precursor to the understanding and applying of the hitherto ignored Behavioural Economics as a study.

In 2017 India is depending heavily on creating opportunities for its youthful 66 per cent population. Our Leaders must provide avenues of opportunities. And young aspiring Indians will not hesitate to convert such opportunities into delivered achievements either- such is the excitement gripping aspiring Indians today!

But these 'opportunities have to be correctly understood and applied by our millions of students, teachers, trainers, managers, entrepreneurs and politicians to create that national synergy. The contents of this book seem to provide some such understanding – an approach to re-learn and **'ignite the fire in the belly**- endorsed by the Late Dr Kalam in his books.

Palit has been one of the thousands of ordinary students from ordinary families, nurtured by me in the course of and out of my role as an academician- a role I covet much more than the corporate role I have had to play before 2005. Each one of my mischievously intelligent ordinary student, including young Palit, has had extraordinary aspirations within them also. I could feel this as I interacted with them, class after class down the years till date.

It is apparent that with Palit and a few others, such aspirations are now slowly blossoming. His first book gives me hopes of a rejuvenated India surely emerging by 2022 under the National Vision for the 75th Anniversary of our Freedom, which even our Prime Minister yearns for...But it needs the will and energy of each and every Indian to become harshly pragmatic, self-disciplined and strategic. This book discusses micro ways and means to managing to hold ourselves and our communities together in this VUCA World. Indeed it almost provides an anti-thesis to the argumentative younger Indians hitherto considered rigid, selfish and inflexible. It provides another way of looking at issues and stimulates the reader to explore the unexplored harsh reality of preparing for 2022.

Partho S. Sengupta

Professor-Behavioural Sciences,
NLP Trainer, Consultant cum
Corporate Mentor

164/A/22 Lake Gardens,
Calcutta 700 045-
partho.sg@gmail.com

Preface

In this book of mine, I have tried to bring out the true meaning of freedom in the context of human thought, economic growth, individual capability and rise in one's conscious level to validate the highest level of knowledge.

I owe my gratitude to my parents for my book and also to our Honourable Prime Minister Shri Narendra Modi sir as this book is in alignment to his thoughts on India Vision 2022 as he brought out in India Today. My sincere thanks also to my professor P.S. Sengupta sir for his thoughts on personal and general revenue improvement programme that has been brought out in the book.

With due respect to **MR TAPAS KUMAR PALIT AND MRS SHAMPA PALIT**

Regards,

SOUMAK PALIT
(Author)

Acknowledgement

I would like to provide my sincere thanks and gratitude to my professor Partho Sengupta sir, our honourable Prime Minister Shri Narendra Modi, the President of India honourable Shri Pranab Mukherjee's book "Thoughts and Freedom" and the management fraternity who has given management principles and practices new thoughts and direction. I have drawn from these living legends their noble thoughts that inspired me to write this book.

Management is not only confined to efficient corporate practices but also to our day to day affairs and the administrative wings of the country in its greater sense. Management has to be practiced scientifically in terms of its process and psychologically in terms of its intent. As a matter of fact, this book of mine is an attempt to follow the methodologies of our ex-President Late Dr APJ Abdul Kalam, who once expressed the dream campaign of India Vision 2020 and its characteristics that will redefine India as a super power in the globe. This book is an attempt to bring a consciousness in the minds of the readers to act as a "change agent" in today's topsy-turvy world which is in full of needs. Invention and creativity as an essence and effective management as a beacon, this book is a blend of tradition with modernity that talks on the soul of management which is quite distinctive and different from traditional management books and theories.

Thanking you and Happy Reading,

Soumak Palit

(Author)

Learning Objectives

(1) A moment's thought for our motherland:-

- We say our government is inefficient if some of our aspirations are not fulfilled.
- We saw our laws and legal system is very rigid and unpractical.
- We say that women are unsafe now a days in our country
- We say our economic system is unable to provide justice to the underprivileged.

We say and say- ***"What are we doing about it?"***

(2) **'PURA' (Providing Urban Amenities to Rural Areas)**, is the essence of activity based management in today's situation. An initiative brought out by the then President of India Late Dr APJ Abdul Kalam, that needs Vedic management to be practiced in true sense, a brain based thinking activity, an attitude towards self-sustainability and greater sense of responsibility as a bonafide citizen.

(3) "Ask What We Can Do and Do What Has To Be Done"- Sir J.F.Kennedy (Ex-President, USA)

(4) "In modern society the more we pursue material improvement, ignoring the contentment that comes from inner growth, the faster ethical values disappear from our communities"-The Dalai Lama

(5) "Talk to yourself at least once in a day…otherwise you may miss a meeting with an EXCELLENT person in this world"- Swami Vivekananda

Your soul is the greatest managerial teacher and mentor for you that inculcates situational based leadership within you.

(6) "Long range planning does not deal with the future decisions, but with the future of present decisions"- Peter Drucker (Management Guru)

Introduction

Life is a gift of almighty. We often wonder why our lives are like it in the present state and then we fall back to our thinking loop which gives us two ways- first, where I am heading towards and what if the things were like the way I wanted, and secondly, sometimes we like to stay in our past and ask God to give back the same joyous state as it was before, in both cases we come across a common war, that is the rational debate that takes place between our mind and heart. One essential thing which we fail to realise or very few of us realises is what are the driving forces behind every step in our lives- is it God's creation and our blind acceptance to it? Or is it that there is certain power instincts by which we can be architect of our lives? The answer lies in the fusion of the chapters which I have presented in my book. The book is centred on "***WELFARE ECONOMICS***" and "***DEVELOPMENT OF INDIVIDUAL***".

Hope, the book will bring development in readers and wish you all a joyous reading.

Regards

SOUMAK PALIT
(Author)

Chapter – 1

Education

Before beginning with my speech, I would like to echo the sayings of Swami Vivekananda-

> "Take up one idea; make that one idea your life, think of it, dream of it, live on idea. Let the brain, muscles, and nerves every part of your body be full of that idea".

In the present era, the concept of "Education" needs to be redefined. To speak in layman's term education is what we learn from our course books and day-to- day sightseeing. But the concept has evolved in the present world of **knowledge management**, and according to me now it is an art as well as science of delivering right values and skills at right place and at right time. It is art in the sense as it involves a degree of creativity in the way an individual acquires the knowledge, to be more precise how they structure their thought process with vast store of information in their brain- a treasure house of knowledge. Knowledge is science in its application that is in what context the given set of information will be applied both consciously or unconsciously, that is triggered by our brain. The success of education lies in efficient knowledge management. So, I will establish the following relationship:-

> EDUCATION= f (Knowledge Management, Self Awareness, Key Attributes defining education)

Another concept which I would like to discuss is the line of difference that is existing between **freedom of mind** to perceive new

(1) Management practices should aim at developing the culture of thought promotion, creating knowledge dynamics and networking through right channels.

(2). Team building should engross the value of diversity in terms of not only gender but also with respect to managing the values of its core functionalities and brand values.

concepts and generate ideas v/s. **mind subjection**, which is resistant to change. The success indicator is that there is a collaborative movement of flow of mind and flow of information which will enable our brain to filter information as per the need of the situation and time and assign weights to it, as a basis of relative importance. So, Education should be time specific and situation specific, in order to use it as core competency and creating it as a strategic asset. The process of education must be capable of fine tuning the behavioural and mind setup of the individuals.

The process of knowledge management and self awareness works together; they are not free standing institutions, an individual's highest level of self awareness relies on the efficiency in the functioning of knowledge management. An individual's **career planning** is the lifeline towards prosperous education and lifelong career growth. The strength of a country's economy lies in the literacy rate of its population and the extent to which they are able to leverage on it. Now, the key attributes defining education that are to be discussed are basically the factors of the external environment affecting education process which includes governmental educational policies, public-private ownership stakes, cultural background of the population. The other side is the internal environment which lies in the human beings itself that is how they channelise their thought process and the way they imbibe the knowledge, that is a proper balance between art of acquiring knowledge and the science of applying it, and to what extent human sentiments and emotions affect information gaining. Education is the outcome of the cultural movement that is prevalent in countries, and culture of any nation is cumulative in terms of its past and present achievements. So, relationship is:-

F(x) = Education=knowledge=Eternity, y= Learning Curve; f(x) =y.

My Suggestions

1. The Need-urgency Theory:—I have developed a theory which I want to discuss is the need-urgency theory. I think it will be a great help to educational policy makers. We need to differentiate between need and urgency.The variables can be used interchangeably, as per

(3). The revenue growth model of an entity should include within its scope the strategic growth factor of the partnering entities, the key components defining the parameters of growth and determining the sustainability factor of it.

(4). Strategy management should not only act as a defender practice but also should stimulate innovation at every step of the organisation life cycle and should act as a differentiator between growth at inception and at maturity.

time and situation for which I mentioned earlier that education should be time specific and situation specific. There is a very simple instance to prove it- we are living in the era of knowledge economy, and we have marched forward from Gen X to Gen Y, which demands "**cross-skilling**" of individuals rather than specialisation in particular field. The need of the hour may be acquiring degrees in engineering, commerce, but the urgency may be that the application phase of knowledge wants a fusion of technical and financial knowledge to be used to come up with a business plan for a company, for instance. Now by focusing on specialisation we are facing the problem of **talent crunch,** as we want that same person to render a particular service but the modern doctrine should be less social investment and maximum output, by encouraging multi-skilling and the cost of extra investment in additional workforce can be used for other projects of the same company to foster growth.

2. Key Attributes Defining Education:—The art acquiring the requisite skills can be defined as "the pathway which an individual undertakes to add marginal benefit to the economy and which can take any shape of an asset that is either generating more money flow in the domestic economy in short run or is capable of earning foreign exchange at long run which may also occur post retirement of an individual if he or she continues to practice their knowledge for the betterment of the community. The scope of education is directly proportional to the utility factor derived from various form of assets which an individual may possess (land, house property and the intellectual ability), all should be taken into consideration. Education is not only confined to institutional qualifications and rendering services to MNCs, they are no doubt an important parameter of educational outcome but there are other parameters also which can be termed as 'self-employment'. It is rather of utmost importance in this era where employment scarcity and poverty has engulfed almost a considerable portion for the developing economies.

3. Redefining Education:—Education in the present context needs to be redefined to give it a proper shape. We can say that "education is the art of creation of the mind in a newer way that is delivering a new set of values both cultural and knowledge wise to create a better community". It is also concerned with creating a

(5). The key to economic planning lies in conceptualising the developmental scope, performing break even on it and nurturing scientific solutions.

(6). The success to learning is centred on deepening the thought process on concept evolution, cultural enrichment, creativity and questioning the status quo.

strategic relationship with other countries, societies in terms of people-to-people perspective. An individual is capable of creating wonders if it can build relations with the outer world and try to unlock the mysteries that are associated with value addition both in terms of economic growth and a higher sense of responsibility and maturity. 'Maturity' can be defined as the capability which an individual shall possess to take current decision on any grounds by keeping in track the influence factor which acts on the foreseeable future. The crux of the matter lies in how far we are able to reduce the gap between certainty and uncertainty and thus, as a result reduce the magnitude of the problems both at the personal level and the national level. Each of us from the time we are born is tied to our country with a debt, a vow to deliver rich values and maintain the nation's spirit by which we as citizens of the country can show it the path to glory. 'Responsibility', on the other hand is more to do with the practical aspect of life compared to 'maturity', which is the thinking aspect. So, we can say:

PERSONALITY= Maturity+Responsibility

Now, the deciding factor is how the maturity criteria can go side by side with the sense of responsibility. Many times in our life journey we are challenged to choose between two options, both seems to be viable. It gives birth to phenomena which we term as ethical dilemma. At such a moment of time, we should calculate the weight of various decisions having right combination of maturity and responsibility. Let me give a very small example, suppose today you are asked by your superior that your performance will be measured in two sets:-

(a) Normal Performance= Day to day yield that an individual is adding to the existing value of the entity. It can be measured by taking the mean average of the individual's performance compared to other entities in the same sector.

(b) Superior Performance= It will be measured in terms of what utility is derived by other sectors from an individual contributing to a particular sector in which he or she is specialised.

Now, the strategy of placing the priority is context specific. It means that with a proper thought process an individual needs track

(7). The issues with leadership lies in setting down proper planning horizon, managing the talent pool, and developing the culture of thinking from baseline.

(8). The main difference between developed and developing economy lies in capturing the economic values of the commons rather than the entire economy as a whole.

which one out of the two parameters will have a greater say in the company's revenue model building depending on what stage of the life cycle (introduction, growth, maturity and decline), the company is operating at that time within the industry.

What Is Learning?

The process of effective learning has three components attached to it:

(1) Defining the attributes and matching the skill sets
(2) Competencies aligned to growth
(3) Is having the adequate resources to share in order to determine the post-learning utility ratio

The post-learning utility ratio will take into account an individual's current status, his adaptive culture to the societal demand and the ability to participate in the developmental process as a change agent.

Traits That A Student Must Possess

1. Individualistic—If a student possess this characteristic, then he or she is in a position to define themselves both at their present level and also how they chalk out their career planning to reach their desired state of satisfaction, with no room for deviation. This question is answerable through self questioning- "What I am, and what can I do?"

2. Dynamism—Now a days we are in the era of Generation Y, where we have redefined the concept of "specialisation", and have marched forward towards the concept of "cross-skilling". The measurement of "Input-Output Ratio", must be in terms of not only to what extent an individual is capable of rendering specialised services in a particular field, but also in terms of to what extent an individual is adoptable to different scenario thinking and conceptualising ideas in practical context, which may include contributions from different fields of study.

3. Core Competency vs. Supplementry Competency:—Its all about going out of your comfort zone and delivering your best. Attitude plays a very crucial role in it as it brings out the true example

(9). The limitations of management lies in performing the "What-if" analysis between the American and Japanese system of management.

(10). The weightage factor associated with managerial tasks of planning, staffing, organizing should not only depend upon the business environment and economic conditions but also on the variations in developing its capability model in alignment with the growth target sustainability.

of transformational leadership within us. Success lies in maintaining a proper balance between the two forces.

4. Emotional Intelligence:—In our learning process, consciously or unconsciously we draw more information by practical experience or by sightseeing and it remains in our memories for much longer time period, rather than by bookish knowledge. Have we ever wondered why it so happens? Let's see it beyond the boundaries of Kolb's Learning Model. We will find a concrete answer- because what we see around in our social circle we have our sentiments attached to it which may be in the shape of either positive or negative vibrations, that enables us to have a better grip over the concepts. So, allow your minds to function as wings of birds.

5. Revenue Improvement vs. Wealth Improvement Programme:—This phase defines education with reference to "going global by being local". The gap between RIP and WIP must be minimised. This can only be done through multi-skilling and also to some extent reforming government's education policies. Reviving the scholarship schemes and allowing students to take part by inviting viewpoints from them etc.

6. Meta Model with Learning:—There is a linear relationship existing between meta modeling and learning as perceived by individuals. It means structure your knowledge in the manner as it renders utility. The outcome of any knowledge must end in test for validity and relevance (Reliability Test).

So, application of knowledge is an art, whereas best-fit of it is science (cause-effect relationship).

Education-utility Theory—Well, after so much of discussion, out of my personal experience I prepared this theory. This theory has two parts- (a) cause-effect relationship, and (b) utility factor attached to it.

The starting point of acquiring of any knowledge is the sense of urgency for it and the logical rationality attached to it. E.g. when an individual thinks and decides between which stream of study they will adopt for their career, there is a constant debate between money driven career prospects and an individual's career liking, which if

(11). The crux of Competency is the ability of an individual to be multi-tasking, adaptable and sensing logic in right path.

(12). The ease from entity's structural rigidity lies in balancing the initiatives of the subordinates with manpower planning and process re engineering to crisis management.

both are in consensus then there is an equilibrium in career prospect, and disequilibrium will result in dis-satisfaction and at times mental retardation and contribution to career development becomes almost nil, and hence there is sharp decline in utility (satisfaction level), and HDI (Human Development Index). When I say about knowledge gaining, I also mean a substantial level of knowledge sharing, in this knowledge economy. By this, there will be rise in marginal utility exchange, and it will rise instead of falling, as every individual has some differentiated talent attached to them, which needs to be nurtured. So, the ideal state of application of this theory would be an existence of inverse relationship between social investment (education) and talent crunch at the international employment market.

(13). The act of significance in context of management lies in developing a culture of win win situation, minimising the gap between where about and what about and creating synergy between knowledge transition and patenting it.

(14). Leadership is not only about being a risk seeker but rather an effective conglomeration of risk balancing and gaining constancy in workflow in terms of strategic approach to creating a concrete relationship management dynamics.

Chapter – 2

The Art of Motivation

When we say about motivation we are usually in a dilemma regarding how to define the scope of motivation. We need to make an analysis about how we do justice to motivation at different point of time. At any point of time our motivation process passes through three stages:

Stage 1–The first phase is how we visualise things, that is are we able to define our limits of growth and our capabilities to reach that point. In this phase we need to imagine the limits within which we are performing our tasks and search the associated paths that can add colours to the process

Stage 2–The second phase, is who the associated partners that are joining the journey to provide a proper shape to the decision making models of an individual which may be in the form of- past experiences giving an edge in the current state or at the future time period, creativity, emotional intelligence to counter the situational issues and the strategic sequencing of the bottlenecks and achievements in an individual's life phase

Stage 3–The final phase, is creating the win-win situation where an individual is able to logically track the factors that define the completeness of his life both in terms of his existence and personal satisfaction

An individual's motivation process is the process of self-reflection of validating knowledge both in static and transformative

(15). Ethical management is not only about focusing on integrity among peer groups but also maintaining the values and virtues of nobility at the time of crisis.

(16). A managerial team's efficiency is not only about chasing a single goal but also it will be great if the team members maintain the exemplary of perfections on one on one basis that is being self driven and attaining measurable goals in the foreseeable future.

form, ranking the social demand in alignment with the societal norms and is able to market his skills in an ethically beneficial manner.

Strategic Motivational Thinking

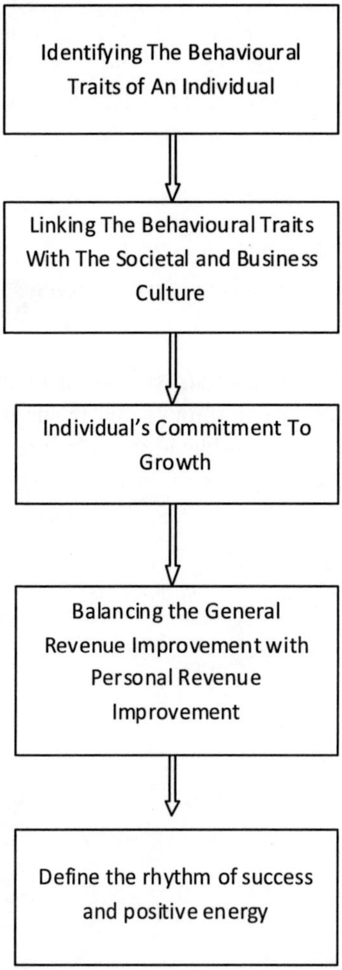

During the Renaissance period, the civilisation was going through a transformation in terms of the lifestyle, attitudinal changes, and knowledge management. People started to act as change agents. The

(17). Creating Team identity should have a positive linkage with the organisation's Employee branding strategies.

(18). The act of administrative dominance should be questioned through determining the levels of competitive advantage in terms of proficiency and clarity of skill profiling and repositioning the scope of micro management.

features with which people started building their success stories are outlined below:-

(1) Defining motivation in alignment to their capabilities
(2) Able to clearly differentiate between key success factors and competency level
(3) Is capable of mapping himself as a strategic asset resource at different levels of organisation's work process
(4) Is capable of successfully leveraging the talent flow as a brand in the global market

Below is the list of questions that an individual at a workplace can ask himself to know where they stand in the process of being an motivated individual.

Questionnaire on Managerial Values Assessment

(1) I act in ways which demonstrate that I am "in charge" —Agree/Disagree
(2) I invest considerable effort in developing others —Agree/Disagree
(3) I recognise outstanding performances —Agree/Disagree
(4) I recruit staff with great care —Agree/Disagree
(5) I treat people with genuine difficulties with compassion —Agree/Disagree
(6) I will always define the performance standards after consulting with my team mates —Agree/Disagree
(7) I take great care to ensure that key decisions are well considered —Agree/Disagree
(8) I help others to develop their careers —Agree/Disagree
(9) I am willing to exercise authority —Agree/Disagree
(10) I deliberately build teams —Agree/Disagree
(11) I always give fair hearing to all parties at the time of disputes —Agree/Disagree
(12) I abide by strict code of conduct —Agree/Disagree
(13) I always analyse the end effect of a particular situation and is not always focused on the current situation —Agree/Disagree

(19). One's conscious approach to work is directly related to its emotional intelligence.

(20). The Goal achievement consists of several inter -related workflows but one's approach to it is highly autonomous in nature which cultivates creativity- an essence of management.

(14) My pride in the job is revenue driven —Agree/Disagree
(15) My pride in the job is ensuring stability —Agree/Disagree
(16) My pride in the job is enjoying autonomy —Agree/Disagree

The critical factor in analyzing the motivational process is to ensure that there exists a proper balance between growth and stability, Eq and Iq, determining the critical path of workflow and flexibility plans and self- branding.

Motivation Mapping

Balancing Time Lag Between Resource Substitutability and Competency Growth	Determining Key Success Factors and Its Share To Economic Value Addition
Crisis Vs. Situational Leadership in Terms of Creating Competitive Barriers	Structuring The Thought Process and Knowledge management techniques (MBO)

CASE 1- A manager can solely take into consideration the first factor of balancing the time lag. This is the situation where an entity is looking towards attending economies of scale and is undergoing the phase of maturity in the organisational life cycle. It will also enable the organisation to attend cost leadership.

CASE 2- The second factor of crisis vs. situational leadership is an all time necessity for entity to sustain. In this phase a HR manager has to critically analyze whether a particular resource is suitable to undergo test in assessment or development center. It has to ensure that skills do not overlap and is able to differentiate between various levels of competencies. In order to follow this factor an entity has to go for preparing Employee Branding report.

CASE 3- The critical incident technique of job diagnosis is the best part of third factor. We need to analyse the nature of outcomes of an individual's goal directed behaviour towards work. The magnitude of change in outcomes and which is the change agent for each process must be taken due care. The favourable outcomes can be in the form of promotion, lesser grievances, favourable input-output ratio, and more flexibility in work process with a feel of autonomy and lesser

(21). Competency Model Development:-

Phase A:	Phase B:
Identifying the knowledge and skills relevancy factor	Developing trends on growth patterns by establishing linkages between span of control and innovation
Phase C:	**Phase D:**
Baselining the critical issues involved in generating a particular competency for making comparative analysis	Bridging the gap of competency limitations existing between manpower transition from assessment to development centres

supervision etc. The change agent can be the organisation training team, OD professionals, or any third party institutions.

CASE 4- The last factor has more to do with societal conventions. Here, an individual has to decide whether he is acting more as a motivator or a facilitator. There can be situation where an economy has adequate knowledge but is failing to leverage on it due to inadequate support structure. For e.g. If we see USA, the population is mostly an aging economy which can mostly act as a motivator rather than facilitator, whether in India the population is more inclined towards youth where the need of the hour is to derive an equal weightage strategy towards setting knowledge gaining procedures, managing cross- cultural conflicts, setting core ideologies and value chain analysis.

(22). Decisional Analysis:-

On Growth:	On Maturity:
Identifying the value proposition and the key success factors associated with it	Focusing on the sustainability factor, strategic map configuration and amalgamations
On Reform:	**On Unique Propositions:**
Consumers spending analysis on the product/services and the possible variations that can be introduced in the offerings	Will the management principles be based on high task variety and low autonomy or will it focus on developing new capabilities

Chapter – 3

Welfare Economy

The present situation in this world especially after globalisation throws challenges on how every country adopts the requirements of the world and configures its economic policies accordingly for inclusive growth and development. The" total utility" generated by an economy at any point of time may not always result in value upliftment of any fraction of population because of two central reasons:-

(1) The demand put forward by international economies may not align to the supply needs of the domestic economy at a particular point of time and thus lead to lag in the form of market competitive forces.

(2) The existing productive manpower of an economy may not always be willing to provide service in the domestic economy and are willing to migrate to other economies that provide better monetary rewards and thus the production is hampered.

The "Economic freedom" is one of the crucial factors that needs to be assessed to judge what is the extent of ownership rights being enjoyed by the under privileged sections of the society and the level of activities that is undertaken by them in sink with the general mass in the process of development.

Welfare Economics And Capability

Welfare Economics can be defined as, "the ways and means that

(23). The essence of developing a holistic business strategy should rest on four pillars:- Capacity Planning, Decisional analysis, Intellectual property protection and maintaining liaison with strategic partners for inclusive growth.

an individual can adopt to move from his current state to enhanced state and simultaneously uplifting the standard of living of the underprivileged sections of the society by creating welfare opportunities for them."

Before, defining capability we need to understand "Demand", in the context of welfare economics. "Demand", can be divided into two parts:-

(1) The average time period for which an individual income earner is able to attain the 'equilibrium stage', by maintaining his income level for meeting the living standard and also the needs of the society (company, or any other practice).

(2) In the long run, we have to look for bridging the gap between the literacy rate and the frequency of growth in the inter-economy employment market. E.g.:- there arises a problem regarding employee substitution and adaptability to different challenges which the economies come up at particular point of time, for which course delivery and tenure must be aligned to the different countries employment laws, migration rules and foreign policies.

In order to meet the above two goals, following conditions must be fulfilled:-

(1) **Literacy Rate**= fraction of population meeting the benchmark/population accessible to education*100

(2) **Choice Set**= comparison between core strength and service asset to capture the utility value.

Service Asset can be defined as, "the list of attributes that are defined by the planning commission pertaining to GDP growth and the set of values that an individual posses to match the requirements at that particular point of time."

(1) The "Capability", is to be measured in terms of 'marginal contribution' that an individual is making to various sectors with the acquired skills and knowledge.

(2) Capability and functioning is not confined to combination of offerings of actual state, rather how much we are leveraging on our freedom and able to explore opportunities.

(24). Learning Modules:-

Module 1 (Introductory)	**Module 2 (Advanced)**
Designing the learning module suppor- ted by what –if analysis of the uncertain issues and management	Analytical vigour should be should be context specific and should gain higher weightage on need analysis by objectives

Economic Freedom:-The term "freedom", can be defined as the quantum of value exchange that an individual is capable of doing in various situations and the ability to analyse them into future growth and stable livelihood building".

The situation specific can be divided into three parts:-

(1) State of normalcy-It is the situation where an individual already has a strong family background to establish themselves in context of the global situation.

   (a) Productive capacity of the family is creating new benchmark to achieve the Pareto constancy for the rest of the population to meet the globalisation challenges of the world economy.

   (b) Pareto Optimality= marginal growth of that particular fraction of population – Marginal utility of the focused group (per cent change inutility/ per cent change in literate population).

(2) State of maturation:-The main focus here is related to quality of education and training imparted by various countries to cater with their economic demands both in the short run and the long run. In this case, the gap analysis is to be made between mean year of acquired education and real time acquired education. Real time is concerned with reaching the development phase of the employment cycle of an individual, while the mean time is concerned with the time frame within which an individual is ready to start its employment cycle.

(3) State of Valuation:-The state where Self demand=Economic Demand.

Where,

Self Demand= Individual's efficiency rate*competency rating growth

Economic Demand= Industry demand in domestic economy and international economy benchmark.

Individual's Efficiency Rate= Marginal Growth of the individual's performance as a result of better training, technological advancement,

(25). Knowledge Economy:-

Module 1 (Introductory)	Module 2 (Advanced)
Segregation of knowledge transition on the basis of aging population in workforce	Identifying the source of knowledge creation for performing a balance act between domestic and international economy requirements
Building a culture of learning by unifying the individual growth targets to economy's necessities	Linking one's talent base to general revenue growth rather than solely on personal growth no my requirements

holistic work environment, one's access to resources + Base level performance.

Competency Rating Growth= various performance weightage given by organisations' on the basis of their life cycle (growth, maturity).

Human Development-The process of human development is the art of three states:-

(a) A position in which an individual is able to define the very basis of his existence by way of value addition to his life and to the society.

(b) Is in a situation where he can extract his demand, even in conservative economic environment where there is employment and money crunch.

(c) is able to amalgamate the output of his domestic economy to the global economy.

Thus, we have to consider the following:-

(1) The time lag between the creation of demand and supply of it.

(2) The elasticity of substitution by the existing resources to contribute towards actual capital and potential capital, relating to GDP Growth.

Human Development Index must consider and compare the cost of growth that an economy is bearing with the value return that various fraction of population is providing both within the economy and in the international economy.

(A) Within the Economy:-

Cost of Growth= (1). Market value of the resource <Cost of acquisition of that resource.

(2). Rate of Inflation > Return on exchange of currencies.

Value Return= The expected years of converting the resource into delivery mode*Utility factor.

Where, Utility Factor= Weighted Average of years of education to enter into employment cycle*Cost associated with it/Total Cost channelised into the sector in the budget by the Government.

(26). An individual's management principles must answer the issues of service through universal acceptance, reviving the spirit of humanity and promoting participative form of administration through which value based ethical management is gained.

(27). Emotional intelligence at work place is not only tested through mind mapping solutions but also through leadership dynamics that one can exhibit at various situations.

(B) International Economy- The value that an individual is able to attract to stabilise the EXIM policy, Balance of payments and increase the frequency of currency exchange in the economy. It can be depicted by the following table:-

Total population of the economy getting migrated to earn foreign exchange	Utility comparison by way of currency flow to mark the trading pattern of the currencies in international money market
Proportion of currency flow by way of core and supplementary competencies	Average Revenue Curve growth must be maintaining a constancy in terms of marginal revenue, marginal cost, target growth rate and monetary policies

Thus, when we are looking into human development we must consider the two factors that contribute towards it:

(1). Growth stability-The challenging factor is whether the government policies is able to maintain stability in terms of employment conversion, education, aging factor utility, job stability.

(2) Growth constancy-The next phase is to ensure that proper benchmarking of standards are met with, creating provisions for economic shocks, skill upliftment experimentation, skill substitution elasticity degree, and economic prosperity.

So, when we talk about welfare economy in real terms we should basically focus on resource mobility in terms of skill up gradation and talent crunch balancing, the magnitude of change that will be brought in terms of economic agreements between developing and developed economies.

(28). Women diversity in managerial positions is not only about reflecting gender diversified workforce but to ensure better emotional stability and safety at workplace.

(29). Process Re-engineering for business development is not only a strategy to mitigate risks but also to stabilise development even in the era of economic uncertainties and adverse situations.

Chapter – 4

Effective Management-Lagaan Way

The movie Lagaan portrays the managerial instincts and characteristics throughout its story. The central theme that it highlighted revolves around leadership strategies, teamwork, emotional intelligence, positive psychology, and adaptability to name a few. The movie also highlights about centralisation vs. decentralisation of authority, system hierarchy, the spirit of collaboration and also to believe on the fact that renovation also plays a vital part along with innovation. The Lagaan movie depicts about diversity management, skill adaptability and how we define leadership in 21st century, the leadership skills that are flexible, strategic and clear cut vision.

Application of Lagaan Match to Johari Window:-

ARENA	BLIND SPOT
ABhuvan's aggressiveness to new thinking Villagers backward approach to lifestyle	Captain Russell's over confidence to win opposed by the Captain Cotton Kachra, proving to be a strategic asset for the team
FAÇADE	UNKNOWN
Bhuvan's confidence of creating history Bhuvan's analytical skills to judge who all will be best fit in the team Ability to adopt to and meet challenges	Captain Russell's hasty decision about the match and support by his team mates resulting in a high pay off for the British Empire

(30). Effective leadership is not only about establishing strong principles of administration but its also about reflecting the voice of the commons.

(31). Developing team spirit is centred around building empathy for fellow members rather than only relying on competitive spirit.

Explanation of Lagaan to Johari Window:-

Case 1- ARENA (Known to others and self)-This phase when we apply to lagan story, we can find that Bhuvan was quite adoptable to new challenges which reflects his skill as a great Situational Leader. He was leading by example and showing the villagers about the need of the hour with lot of positive energy within him and also used the technique of rational persuasion to stand for a common cause of saving the drain of wealth, thus defining the vision statement.

Case 2- BLIND SPOT (Known to others, not to self):-Captain Russell was a man who enjoyed complete bureaucratic style of administration. As a leader he lacked in analysing a particular decision from different angles (critical aspects of decision making), a true example of a person who practices Machiavellians in an organisation as we can find that the captain was spontaneously taking decisions without interacting with the higher authority as opposed by Captain Cotton and Major Warren. Kachra, the spinner from backward class was accepted by Bhuvan and recognised inspite of awkward feeling of the villagers, which reflects Bhuvan's quality of rational persuasion, proper skill management technique where his aim was to acquire the right talent in the team and commitment to achieve a shared goal.

Case 3- FAÇADE (Not known to others, known to self):-The central character of the movie Bhuvan was always optimistic about his decision and was high on all three dimensions of emotional intelligence-self-awareness (knowing the cause of the action, as was said in the movie that it was not a mere cricket match), self-management (as Bhuvan was focused on what he wants to pursue, though there were negative comments from the villagers at the beginning, he managed Lakha during the critical phase of the game which is an exemplary of crisis leadership), and social skills (as inspite of going against the British, he agreed to take the help of Queen Elizabeth for learning the game of cricket, which shows he is situation-oriented, and have a strong sense of feelings towards the demand of time).

Case 4- UNKNOWN (Not known to others and self):-Captain Russell is a classic exemplary of negative side of optimism which resulted in a vague challenge that he created (to pay the Queen three

(32). Managerial Effectiveness Practice:-

Channelizing growth through the key competency areas which the organization can leverage upon as strategic assets	Proper alignment between organizational restructuring at business level as well as operational level with equal weightage to sub functional units at the time of innovation
An entity's expansion policies must point out the solution of best fit in a different economy's market structure which can be quite different	Human capital development must focus on setting up differentiation skill strategies as per competency cluster and enhancement of talent

times the tax), there was no specific goal setting direction for him and just played luck by chance. In the motivation process, he ranks high on Need for Power rather than Need for Achievement.

Managerial Quality Comparison:-

TRAITS	JUDGEMENTAL FACTOR
Building Task Structures	Bhuvan's Team Management Techniques and Leading by Example
Team Maturity	Britishers were high on it as they were in the commanding position
Analyser and Prospector (Miles And Snow Strategy)	Bhuvan was adaptive to meet challenges and also an opportunity seeker
Managing Culture (Socialisation)	Bhuvan taught the villagers how to sustain cultural differences and promote value (talent management)
Recognising Talents	Bhuvan was actually practicing self-externalisation, that is he wanted to see that spirit of winning in everyone's eyes like him, like a leader sees in his team
Knowledge Management	Bhuvan's coordination and networking to Elizabeth to learn the game of cricket in an efficient way and to entertain diverse view points and feedback
Trust	Bhuvan was successful as a servant leader to win the trust of the villagers to make a complete team towards a shared vision

Take Aways From Bhuvan's Leadership Style:-

(1) Is the emotional support provided is sufficient to promote shared vision

(2) Will I allow third party interventions to promote my goal

(3) Do I provide a fair chance to culturally diverse workgroup in all activities

(4) Am I always a risk taker or do I hold every team mate equally responsible

(5) Is my leadership consulting in nature or deals with authority

(6) Do people follow me obediently or do I have to undergo conflict

(33). Management Principles:-

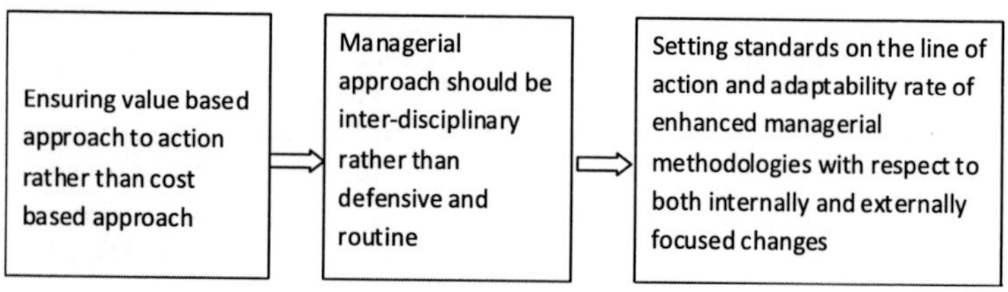

(7) Do I create a win-win situation for my subordinates at all times

(8) Do I allow people to humiliate and be assertive towards me

(9) While taking decision do I always count on past inferences or like to be innovative in nature

(10) I am always compassionate toward others and do not like to exhibit bossicism

(34). EQ and IQ Test:-

Over viewing the pros and cons of positioning oneself as an effective leader in eyes of subordinates	Maintaining a balance act in cognitive activities in terms of the objectivity and psychological factor
Is understandable and tries to create scenarios where as a leader one's thought process matches to that of his peers	Drives the team to achieve excellence by motivating them in adverse scenarios by using logical judgements and self consciousness

Chapter – 5

Cost-benefit Analysis of Training Programme

Cost Benefit analysis or CBA determines the strategic value development in an individual from training programme and scheduling the resource value chain in order to achieve the desired outcomes. It is also to do with balancing the returns received on manpower investment, skill substitution and the cost of resources associated with it. CBA enables the decision maker to make a rational choice from talent generation schemes, cost-benefit analysis and resources mapping that help the trainer to judge not only what will be gained but also the value of the resources that will be sacrificed to achieve these gains that is the opportunity cost of business value creation and knowledge driven economy building.

Cost Benefit Valuation

The valuation of benefits and costs should reflect preferences revealed by choices which have been made. The most challenging part of CBA is finding the trends in development associated with economic gains, nation's output building and crisis management. The deciding factor is the marginal benefit must be greater than the marginal cost of the programme, which is the value addition made to the trainee's existing KSAs (knowledge, skills and attributes) to reach the desired level of outcome which will suit the job specifications, task structure and marginal cost that is extra monetary outflow that

(35). Leadership Styles Questioning Facts:-

Authoritative Leader- How to maintain a balance between adhocratic and bureaucratic organisation structure?	*Responsive Leader*- Extent of autonomy provided to team mates and the degree of flexibility, turn around time to implement strategic workflow
Crisis Leader- Ranking and weightage provided to various issues to be solved and impact analysis on the functionalities having linkages	*Servant Leader*- Establishing accountability and ownership and being answerable to the stakeholders round the clock

an organisation incurs as a result of conducting the training programme. The success of any training programme can be quantified against the following parameters:

(1) Resource Management and Configuration- Determining the current strength of the resources- manpower, finance, technology, marketing and sales, service development and distribution channels and mapping the positioning effect with brand market premium.

(2) Resource Asset Generation- Generating and evaluating the resources in terms of its importance (ranking as per the strategic asset of the organisation) and determining the relative strength of its resources in terms of the industry that is to say identifying and quantifying the average lifetime value creation of the resource and tenure of its fluctuation in terms of the global economy.

(3) Training and Knowledge management- It shall deal with the industry workflow cycle management that includes developing the learning environment, criteria setting for the training standards- defining the core and supplementary competencies, balancing economic needs with organisational position in competitive market, framing control charts to determine the expected work flow status and decisional framework with talent management and contractual ratification . The management of key success factor can be of three types:-

Level 1- Ability to analyse the scope of general revenue improvement and performing a diagnosis of the path goal strategic plan stability.

Level 2- The next level is the degree of adhocracy vs. bureaucracy an individual can allow in his team. It has to ensure proper configuration of the knowledge sharing plan, degree of responsibility to be bestowed to his associates vis a vis skill substitution opportunities available, determining the critical path of work flow, importance more on structural decision making (procedural knowledge) or on declarative knowledge (traditional decision making) and determining

(36). Corporate Challenges:-

Degree of sustainability achieved with respect to current legal and economic laws	Level of dependency of earning brand premium on market penetration rather than waiting for favourable business climate
Capital restructuring and financial stability factor at times of amalgamation and merger	Determining the composition of human capital with respect to rational decision for improving efficiency

the quality cycle of the average degree of knowledge as an intellectual property is present in the teams.

Level 3- The final level is to deal with work culture enrichment, fulfill the service quality enhancement motives, identifying the key success factors in employees that is developing the intellectual base of the organisation, performing employee branding in alignment with work flow capability development reporting and performing the skill visibility test of teams in the industry and also in the global market.

Education is a social and economic investment in human beings. There has been a lot of argument as to whether cost-benefit analysis is applicable to education, because of the validity of educational objectives, and importance of its contribution to GDP growth. But now as the investment in education is found to produce significant economic benefits, the need to analyse the nature and magnitude of these benefits in relation to costs must also be recognised along with the time lag in deriving the demand to meet the gap in developing the talents from its nascent stage and up skilling the talents to the delight needs.

Measurement of Cost Factor in Education Programme

The **'cost of education programme'** includes all real resources, thus money expenditures represents:

(a) Purchase of teachers' labour

(b) School buildings and equipments

(c) Learning materials and books

(d) Guest lectures on various subjects

(e) Value of student's time measured in monetary terms

However, there are certain costs which are not reflected in normal expenditures. Example- the students themselves, who deprive the labour, market of their services by choosing to continue their education. This represents a loss of productive capacity, loss of current output for the economy, as well as loss of earnings for the individuals. This loss of present income is one of the opportunity costs of education,

(37).

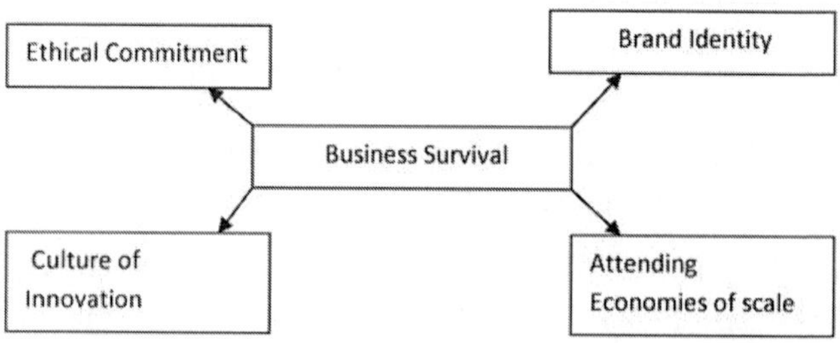
Ethical Commitment
Brand Identity
Business Survival
Culture of Innovation
Attending Economies of scale

as it represents sacrifice of real resources, even though the time of students is not reflected in actual expenditure. Thus,

Cost of Education= The Curriculum cost + Opportunity cost of alternative opportunities foregone either by the student or society as a whole.

The measurement of benefit is in terms of enhancement of KSAs and how efficiently a student is able to correlate his understandings to practical scenarios **(Declarative Knowledge)** and apply the learned concepts in real life situations, the scientific approach to knowledge **(Procedural Knowledge).** The highest level of knowledge is **Validation**. So, at a glance we can see the following benefits which are to be procured from MBA programme:-

(1) The KSA (knowledge, skill and attributes) enhancement in a student

(2) Defining his value statement, whether in alignment with the entity's vision and mission

(3) Analysing the critical aspects of organisational live case studies

(4) Students are capable of performing need analysis in sync with the competencies held and needed by the organisation (Gap Analysis)

(5) Developing a win-win situation through proper peer to peer relationship, knowledge management and succession planning

Steps in Cba Analysis:-

(1). Defining the referent group-The first step is to define the target group of trainees. In this step the organisation needs to define the age group, numbers of years spend in the organisation, personal aim of the trainee and his demand in the organisation, past achievements and the versatility factor in terms of contribution to different organisational functionalities and also the gender composition in terms of talent diversity.

(2) Developing Training Modules-In this step the trainer has to decide the methodology of training- case studies, role plays,

(38).

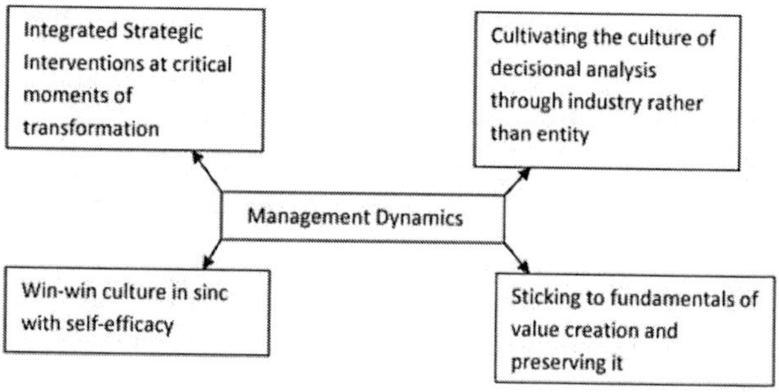
Integrated Strategic Interventions at critical moments of transformation
Cultivating the culture of decisional analysis through industry rather than entity
Management Dynamics
Win-win culture in sinc with self-efficacy
Sticking to fundamentals of value creation and preserving it

simulations, third party institutions, depending on the criticality of the role involved and the organisational standings in terms of its offerings, strategic diversification, market share portfolio, constancy in its growth rate and institutionalisation of its training modules in terms of its affiliations in the international market.

(3) Identify the potential impacts-As training activities goes on role based strategies so the potential impact of the training on general revenue improvement must be assessed. The objective of the training programme may be multi-fold- performance improvement, process reengineering, differentiating between generic and key competencies, benchmarking threshold limits of skills, new practice adaption, skill substitution effects, manpower transitions and immigrations, will the training contents remain valid for long term and if so what shall be the X-factor and will it impact the national or global economy?

(4) Monetary Implications of Training-At the end of the day, what counts for all activities is revenue. One needs to ensure whether the training programme is focused more at strategic level or at operational level. The expectation from the senior management may be- leveraging the talent, lesser supervision resulting in promoting another work process which is very much nische in the market, ensuring cost leadership, and work force composition diversification to gain competitive advantage.

(5) Perform Sensitivity Analysis-This step deals with contingency management. The challenge is how the leadership team assigns weights to different variables impacting organisation which are quite uncertain in nature. The uncertain factors may include- amendments in the provisions of the Contract Act and Business laws around the world or country-specific, recession, political tensions, and other compliances (accounts reporting techniques). Therefore, the need of the hour is to keep an open door policy towards assessing partnerships, leveraging and aligning the key success factors for shared growth and prosperity, and

(39).

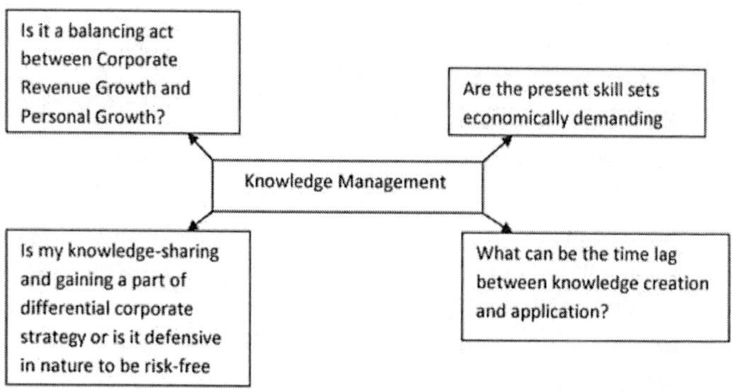
Is it a balancing act between Corporate Revenue Growth and Personal Growth?
Are the present skill sets economically demanding
Knowledge Management
Is my knowledge-sharing and gaining a part of differential corporate strategy or is it defensive in nature to be risk-free
What can be the time lag between knowledge creation and application?

defining the dimensions of value generation by clearly defining the touch points of competitive diversification strategies.

Now, I have taken as an instance MBA programme CBA analysis to study the impact:-

Cost Classification in MBA Programme:-

(A) Direct Costs:-

(a) Tuition Fees
(b) Student Health Fees
(c) Learning Materials and Library fees
(d) Teachers' salaries
(e) Lab fees/E-Resources fees
(f) Admission Fees
(g) Other Institutional Fees
(h) Hostel fees
(i) Mess fees
(j) Utility fees

(B) Indirect Costs:-

(a) Charges for inviting guest lecturers
(b) Cost of holding seminars and conferences
(c) Cost incurred in sending students to educational tour

(C) Developmental Costs:-

(a) Cost incurred for on-the job training
(b) Cost of designing the MBA course which includes classroom training with the help of videotapes, case study printed materials, and cost of examination fees

(D) Compensation Costs:-

(a) Scholarships for the merit list students
(b) Re-exam cost for back papers in semesters
(c) Students looking for off-campus placement

(40).

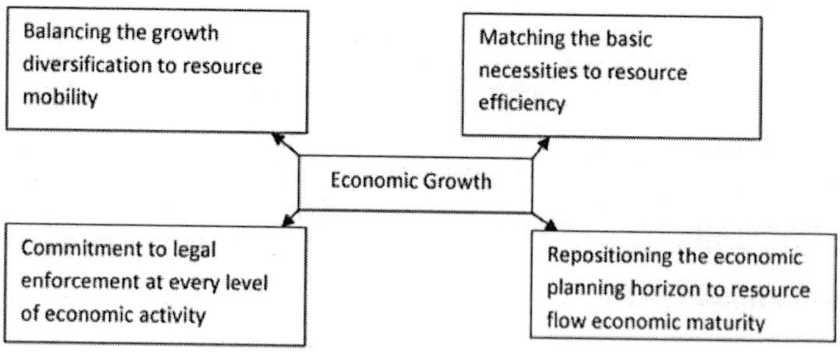
Balancing the growth diversification to resource mobility
Matching the basic necessities to resource efficiency
Economic Growth
Commitment to legal enforcement at every level of economic activity
Repositioning the economic planning horizon to resource flow economic maturity

Utility Mapping After MBA:-

PRE-MBA		POST-MBA	
Communication Ability	–	Communication Ability	–
Analytical Skills	–	Analytical Skills	–
IQ	–	IQ+EQ	–
Declarative Knowledge	–	Strategic Knowledge	–
Leadership Inclination	–	Crisis vs. Situational leadership	–
Preconceived notion on Profit Maximisation	–	Wealth Maximisation	–
Bureaucratic style Leadership		Servant Leadership blend towards CSR	
Revenue Improvement Programme		Amalgamation for shared growth prospects	
Market Growth and Autonomy		Market Growth, Autonomy and Penetration	

The training module of corporate are inclined towards three pillars that is knowledge branding, strategic competitive cutting edge and resource mobility that will enable to fetch rich dividend in the form of stakeholders wealth management, diversifying market portfolio and increasing market growth, corporate identity management, creating strategic partnership for stabilising growth and development and acting as prospectors in seeking global opportunity for attending economies of scale.

(41).

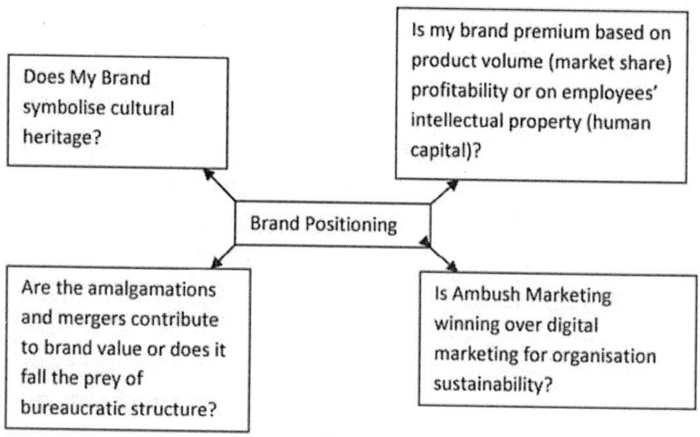
Does My Brand symbolise cultural heritage?
Is my brand premium based on product volume (market share) profitability or on employees' intellectual property (human capital)?
Brand Positioning
Are the amalgamations and mergers contribute to brand value or does it fall the prey of bureaucratic structure?
Is Ambush Marketing winning over digital marketing for organisation sustainability?

Chapter – 6

Vision and Mission- Key Success Factor

"When you have come to this world, try to leave some mark behind, otherwise where is the difference between you and the trees and the stones, they also come, live and decay" – **Swami Vivekananda**

We are often engulfed with a challenge in our life as to how we will be able to set up a comprehensive strategy in terms of building a vision and most importantly living on it. There are cases where people dream of things they want to accomplish but the challenge that they are often confronted with is the time frame of that achievement in this competitive world as everything is demanded to be come in with pace. Our mind intellect always provides us with rich source of nourishment of what our predecessors and our civilisation has left for us to be valued and also have sufficient reasons to value. Why we deviate from our vision and mission is the greatest evil that is resulting in giving birth to a corrupt society in India. A person's quality of vision always gives an insight about his behavioural characteristics and his ability to face up different situations of life. So, basically success lies in how we are able to create a process of smooth interaction between our soul and the external forces that drive the society.

We can define vision and mission in today's context. Vision can be defined as not only deciding of what is to be achieved but also deciding on the weightage of the pros and cons associated with deciding on a particular path. While a mission is concerned with how it is to be achieved, due consideration must be given to the impact of that particular path of achievement as to whether it is benefiting the common mass as to creating a civilised society. So, the scope has

(42).

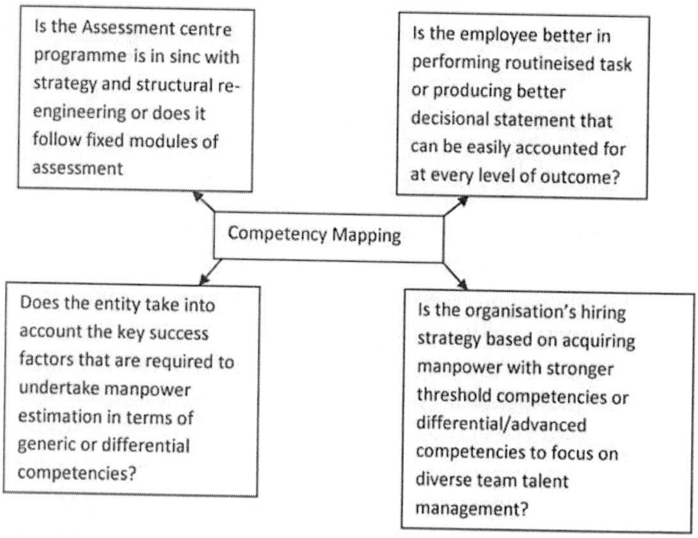
Is the Assessment centre programme is in sinc with strategy and structural re-engineering or does it follow fixed modules of assessment
Is the employee better in performing routineised task or producing better decisional statement that can be easily accounted for at every level of outcome?
Competency Mapping
Does the entity take into account the key success factors that are required to undertake manpower estimation in terms of generic or differential competencies?
Is the organisation's hiring strategy based on acquiring manpower with stronger threshold competencies or differential/advanced competencies to focus on diverse team talent management?

become much wider from micro to macro level as vision and mission defines an individual's attitude towards life which in turn helps a successful civilisation to flourish.

Steps in Building A Successful Vision and Mission:

(1) Asking questions to self regarding its existence, as to how it can create a difference in the society

(2) Making a valuation of all possible areas where it can render utilities

(3) Assessment of KSAs' (knowledge, skills and attributes) aligned to career path

(4) Focus on balancing self growth vs. societal growth to emerge as a star performer

(5) Defining the magnitude of change as to level of consistency, key supportive areas (cultural barriers, financial backup, thought flow process, knowledge management) and family background.

(6) Creating a balance between core competency and supplementary competency to differentiate skills at time of needs and creating differentiation level of performance management.

Process Of Self Realisation:-

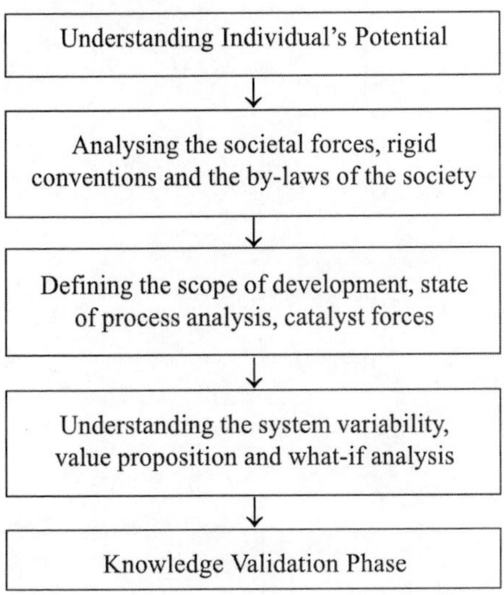

(43). The crux of developing training module lies in analysing the cause and effect relationship between learning intensity and weightage provided to various parameters of learning; the position of the entity in the lifecycle- growth or maturity and target propositions set by the entity in near future.

The steps mentioned above are explained below to provide an understanding of the process flow of self-realisation.

- Understanding Individual's Potential:-Today when we talk about individuals potential we try to get the answer out of the potential human capital and the untapped talent base that lies in the economy. The challenge lies in trapping what part of the total workable population is capable of acting as a "change agent", enabling to take a transformation in terms of activities, skills, processes and life in a collective way.
- Analysing the social forces, by-laws:- The social forces always plays a dominant role especially in India. The challenges which faces us today is our traits aligned to societal betterment when the external forces may act as catalyst or adverse growth. The freedom of thought and action renders utility by configuring the traits as per the society conventions and creating an effective communication channel between art of self management practices which follows a set of valuable lifestyle approach and the opportunities that are provided by the economies around the world.
- Defining the scope of development, process analysis and catalysts:-The entire life of a human being passes through a system that provides a framework of human intellect, shared vision, growth mapping and the diversity of action that an individual needs to adopt to maintain a high level of efficiency. The catalyst forces can be internal or external in nature depending on the state of mind that draws nourishment from the learning process, value system and the motivational forces.
- Understanding the system variability, what-if analysis:-This issue lies in equality with Maslow's need for hierarchy theory. As an individual moves higher from safety needs to social needs to self-actualisation needs the driving forces that shape the process of growth must be configured as per the earning potentials, resource constraints, lifestyle challenges; the driving forces includes age factor, behavioural issues, learning process, aptitude etc. The what-if analysis is

(43).

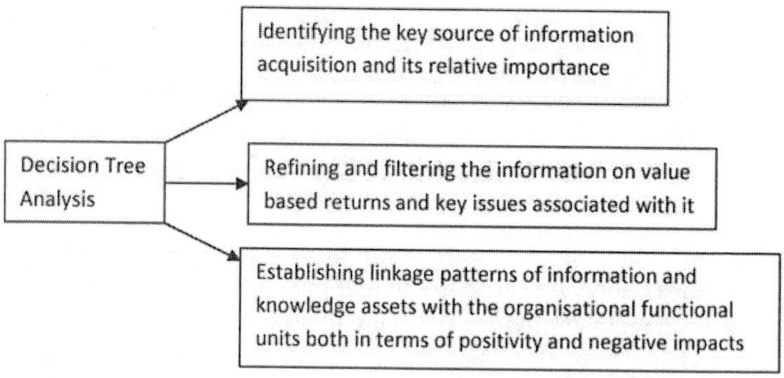
Identifying the key source of information acquisition and its relative importance
Decision Tree Analysis
Refining and filtering the information on value based returns and key issues associated with it
Establishing linkage patterns of information and knowledge assets with the organisational functional units both in terms of positivity and negative impacts

concerned with answering the contextual issues, barriers in terms of resource accessibility and individual capability and people management skills.

- Knowledge validation phase-The key issues addressing the learning process is the learning methodology, sources of acquiring them, and preparing the intellectual base of the economy as invested in building the human capital. The skill substitutability is directly proportional to the investment made in the education system, learning infrastructure availability and knowledge management practices followed.

Thus, knowledge management is the key to successful outcome in this world. Knowledge in today's context not only deals with exploring the sources of acquiring them but also with the art of creating connectivity as all the systems in this world interacts with each other to keep up the momentum of holistic understanding.

Knowledge Management= Creativity + Managerial Skills

(45). The state of art of management deals with the designing element of the activity path analysis and the scientific path deals with determining the causal effect of each path goal dimensions.

Chapter – 7

Competency Management

Competency is the process of identifying, creating and developing intellectual base of an economy either by enabling permanent change in behaviour or through updation in value chain.

A permanent change in behaviour may be caused due to aptitude, skills and attitude. Aptitude is an ability of an individual to act logically towards a given situation which tests ability to think, proper scheduling of tasks and tracking the connectivity that will provide solutions to similar type of issues. Skills have more to do with communication, subject knowledge, and experience. Thus, competency is:

(1) It is a path to defining human talent

(2) It is a cushion to solve issues on skill substitutability and division of labour

(3) Competency development is a combination of skills, aptitude and behaviour

(4) Competency has not only to do with base learning but also deals with all the steps of value addition that an individual makes in his career path

Importance of Competencies:-

(1) Competency provides an insight into the work dimensions critically, job limitations and performance scaling

(46).

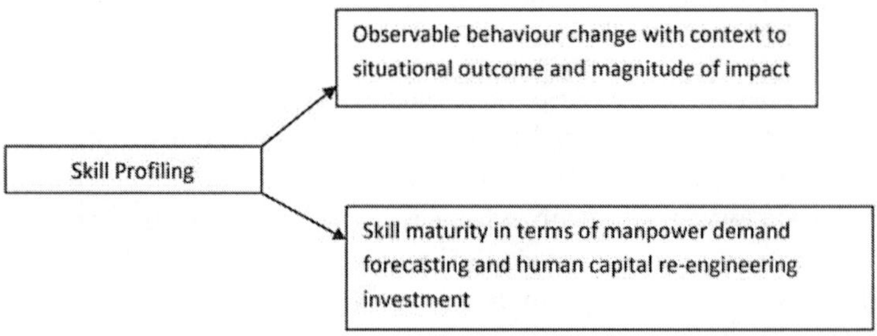
Observable behaviour change with context to situational outcome and magnitude of impact
Skill Profiling
Skill maturity in terms of manpower demand forecasting and human capital re-engineering investment

(2) Competency mapping acts as a differentiating factor in determining workforce capability mapping to assessment or development centre

(3) Competency acts as a cushion in succession planning in an organisation and also acts as a ready reference to solve issues on skill substitution

(4) Competency mapping is also an effective way to undergo organisation restructuring, business process re-engineering and creating USPs (unique selling proposition) for the entity

(5) Competency management enables in "Employee Branding", an essence in today's corporate world

(6) Competency is not pre-defined; it is a balance between career-orientation of an employee and the changing nature of the organisations ultimately contributing to organisation's philosophy

Phases of Competency Development:-

Introductory Stage	***Growth Stage***
Getting overall view of the field of study, its application and limitations in the area of concentration	Analysing the core competencies and supplementary competencies and benchmarking them
Maturity Stage	***Decline Stage***
Determining the key success factor, defining the magnitude of performance measurement (assessment vs. development centre)	Highlighting elements of job through diagnosis that are critical in nature and re defining the value statement through brand repositioning

The above grid provides a picture of how the process of competency management goes on as the organisation passes through the life cycle. The value proposition and the community building that takes place vary as organisation passes through various phases.

Nature of Competencies:-

(1) Motives: -It defines the value statement of an individual that stimulates a course of action. It is goal directed and enables to locate the factor that aligns competencies to career path.

(47).

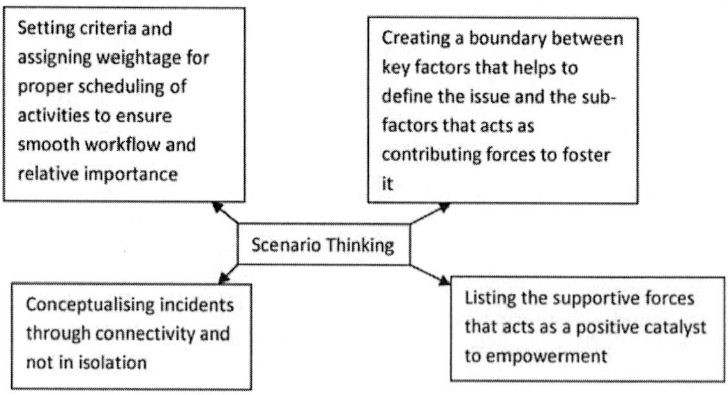
Setting criteria and assigning weightage for proper scheduling of activities to ensure smooth workflow and relative importance
Creating a boundary between key factors that helps to define the issue and the sub-factors that acts as contributing forces to foster it
Scenario Thinking
Conceptualising incidents through connectivity and not in isolation
Listing the supportive forces that acts as a positive catalyst to empowerment

Situational leaders and crisis leadership are best examples of strong motives.

(2) Self-Concept:-This deals with how an individual projects himself to the outside world. Personal beliefs, cultural values, societal regulations linked to business practices are key to act as a catalyst contributing towards self image of a person.

E.g.:-A general entrepreneur's approach towards a managerial decision making will be quite different from that of a rural entrepreneur.

(3) Traits:-It is concerned with the characteristics of an individual that measures his worthiness towards an activity. It can result in the form of IQ, EQ, communication skills, team work, motivation, visionary etc.

(4) Knowledge:-Knowledge has to do with information management, tracking the right sources of information transfer, its applications and leveraging on it. Knowledge can be acquired through various modes- classroom training, on job training, case study analysis, business games, role plays and behavioural event interviews.

(5) Skills:-The ability of an individual to carry out a task. It can be knowledge related, or related to emotional intelligence.

Types of Competencies:-

(1) Core Competencies:-It consists of the basic ingredients that are required to be eligible to be considered as part of human capital asset of an organisation. The competency ranges from communication skills, subject area knowledge, basic computer knowledge etc.

(2) Functional Competencies:-This competency is linked to Henry Fayol's management principle "division of labour". It highlights the uniqueness lying in an individual that acts as a differentiating factor. Functional competency ranges from marketing, operations, finance, IT etc.

(3) Behavioural Competencies:-This competency is a reflection of learning outcomes. The outcomes can be in the form of change in thinking approach, involvement of sentiments

(48). Human Resource management is more of a mind game rather than only ensuring proper employees grievance redressal.

backed by logical judgement in decision making, better peer to peer relationship and conflict management.

(4) Threshold Competencies: -The competencies that are required to perform a job effectively. E.g.:- basic knowledge on C and C ++ for a programmer.

(5) Differentiating Competencies:- The factors that differentiate great performers from average performers. It will consist of factors that enable an individual to create an effective linkage between the systems and create a sound work flow model.

Mathematical Model: Linking Competency and Reward:-

The compensable factor of competency is the standard deviation of the work related activities required to move up to superior performance from average performance.

Superior performance= per cent benchmarked as target performance + base salary*job ingredients weightage

Performance Benchmarking:-

The following steps are required to be taken due care of while designing performance metrics:-

- Designing job performance dimensions as to say the task criticalities, talent configuration, preparing employee base
- Measuring arrears in job growth vs. talent availability
- Designing models on policy gap, bridging the regulatory factors, social barriers, economic issues
- Succession planning both at unit level and corporate level
- Aligning salient features on employee branding as decided by the organisation to its incentive plans and growth targets

The organisation has to quantify the linkages existing between the following groups:-

- Brand premium value and the core strategic intent
- Correlation relationship existing between skill change and process re-engineering
- Knowledge management to leadership development
- Service differentiation to key success factors identification

(49). Competency building and knowledge management are the two critical assets of building a knowledge economy.

- Strategic barriers to entry to value chain analysis
- Marketing the core competencies to stabilising the talent base

Now, the below chart reflects the competency movement as per the expectancy theory of organisational behaviour.

Case A	Case B
Skill Development Assessment of Value Chain Normalisation of Risk Factor	Movement Towards Lean System Skill Development: Change Agent TQM Practices Efficiency
Case C	**Case D**
General vs. Personal Revenue Balancing Diversity to Knowledge Management "What-if Analysis" of Competency	Strategising Cost Leadership Economic Value Addition To Competency Mapping Aligning Growth To Industry Barriers

The above chart gives us a holistic picture of the different stages of development that an individual or an organisation thrives to achieve at different level of activity scheduling. The core strategic intent remains the hub, around which the above factors act as a catalyst to nurture growth and create a win-win situation in the context of both personal growth and enrichment of the organisation philosophy.

Thus, competency is the value that enables an organisation to define its capabilities, success factors, competitive advantages and value proposition that in turn helps an organisation to enrich the value of its vision.

(50). Principles of skill divisibility is directly proportional to manpower skill substitutability.

Chapter – 8

Management Thought: Insight to Practices

In this chapter I shall bring out the traditional management practice linkages to Swami Vivekananda's speech at world parliament of religions at Chicago, 10 Commandments of Bible and Tagore's Gitanjali.

The essence of management lies in the fact that there exists contradictions and difference in the value system that creates different scenarios to manage. Managerial implications finds its source and is centred around how the different stages of human activities draws its relationship from its ancestral civilisation, societal conventions and the challenges imposed by the factors governing the world in the form of legality, economy and people to people development. The crux of the matter lies in core principles of governance, business system, flexibility to dynamism, learning culture and past legacies. Since independence, the challenge with the Indian governance structure is that it revolves around the principle of conservatism, tradition, structural rigidity in terms of bureaucracy and frequent unrest in political climate which undermines the key ingredients of growth and value addition to the society at large.

The scope of efficient managerial practices is centred on five key potentials that are a reflection to human thought process. They are:

- Art of self-realisation

(51).

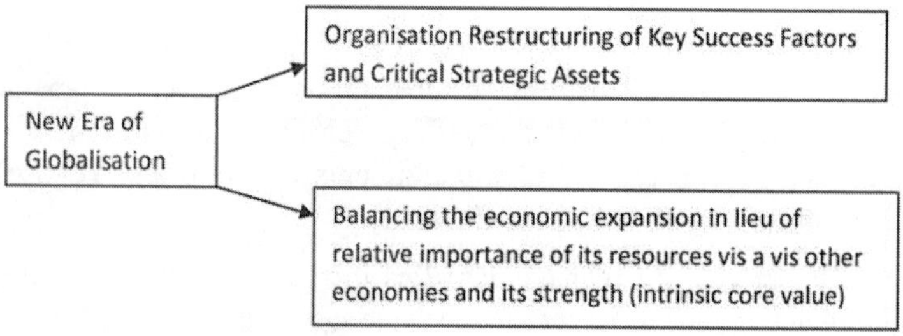
New Era of Globalisation
Organisation Restructuring of Key Success Factors and Critical Strategic Assets
Balancing the economic expansion in lieu of relative importance of its resources vis a vis other economies and its strength (intrinsic core value)

- Talent management practices
- Key competencies aligned to organisation's vision
- Conflict management
- Principles of justice linked to individual beliefs

Art of Self-Realisation:-This phase deals with standing out as a spiritual warrior. The concept of charismatic leadership revolves around it. Management as a religion provides us a source of nourishment by helping us realise the fact of self motivation, team spirit, knowledge management, general revenue improvement, work force mobility and cultural renaissance by practicing universal toleration as said by Swami Vivekananda in his Chicago speech. The outcome of it is to create a win-win situation. The thought of management has evolved through the passage of time for which the major contributors can be:

(a) Human Intellect
(b) Work force diversity
(c) Change in human beliefs through cultural advancement
(d) Adaptability and responsiveness to ever changing environment and re-configuring the limitations
(e) The art of self realisation within the ethical system lies in potential form which gets reflected on a situational basis. So every time there is a creation and human civilisation aligns to that change by acting as a change agent a compound in nature, as stated in Swami Vivekananda Chicago speech.

Talent Management Practices:-Perception plays a key role in the process of learning and adapting to the learning culture. Contradictions are necessary for refinement of thought processes and ultimately to validate the knowledge. Knowledge can be at a nascent stage, transformation stage or at validation stage depending upon the context and the content of managing the information lines. This process demands promotion of talent management practices. Skill availability and skill variability needs to be balanced at all phases of knowledge growth. India is a country where till today a significant portion of human capital remains untapped due to economic imbalance, external relations, geographical limitations and political unrest.

(52). Learning should be experimental rather than merely relying on seeking information.

(a) Knowledge at nascent stage:-It deals with the analysis of the source of knowledge that is to say whether it is a regular source of information flow (schools, colleges, professional institutes) or something which comes on ad hoc basis that is to say by way of practical exposure or by establishing linkages between different fields of study. With context to management, knowledge management scope will include the timely management of information, maintaining stability in thought process, conceptualisation of the value chain of knowledge and building of the learning community and culture.

(b) Knowledge at Transformation Stage:-It is the phase where every base of information revolves around the outcome of change agent attitude. Transformation shall include within its scope management of value propositions, work flow cycle, peer to peer relationship, economic value addition and creating competitive advantage as to branding the talent resource to manage the skill substitution. The transformation stage is an implication of the judicious utilisation of the principle of philosophy of rights and duties to balance the system of management, honouring the moral, ethical and thought flows in a constructive manner among peers. As God is the ever active providence who governs the entire human system being evolved out of chaos as per Swamiji, similarly management also provide nourishment about the cultural heritage, our individual value system, our relationship to the community at large and most importantly how we balance the system to support growth within the pre defined limits.

(c) Knowledge Validation Stage:-This phase is concerned with transformation of the intermediary knowledge into an act of tendency which is demonstrative in nature. It is in totality deals with aptitude building which can take within its form two ways. One in the form of matter materialism that is the existence and linkages of knowledge to the existing situations and its implications. The other can be of the spontaneous nature where there exists a physical configuration of the

(53). Outcome of human sentiments are based upon on past retaliations rather than what an individual seeks to accept and understand.

mind mapping solutions through which a conscious mind acts in a logical way to answer the what-if analysis counterparts. So, it finds its very existence in the wordings of Swami Vivekananda, as he remarked that tendencies of mind and body are two parallel lines of existence similarly management strategy and managerial implications are two parallel lines of existence contributing to effectiveness in a holistic manner.

Key Competencies Aligned To Organisation's Vision:-It lays down the foundation stone of unity in diversity. Failure or striving to reach the point of success is often construed as an act of ignorance. As man is given the potential power to realise his divine nature he is actually gathering more and more strength which begets personal limitations to align it to common intensions to thrive towards a particular vision. As said by Swamiji a successful vision aligned to a successful team can be termed as an attempt of undeveloped minds to grasp high spiritual truths. The spiritual truth here is the service towards development of a common goal where mutual interests align to build a sustainable world. It's a common matter that success stories revolve around assimilation of thoughts and any divergence requires adaption which is again a test of human intellect. Clarity in a vision should be subject to elimination of subjectivism existing in the people which are a showcase of their defensive character.

Thus Vision is:

- Clarity in terms of thought flow
- Building a congenial work culture
- Creating a win-win situation in peer relationship
- Establishing growth stability to value chain blueprint

Management Science: Linking Drucker's Concept To Bible and Gita:

The act of management is socialistic in nature. Management functionalities revolve around human interactions where the key success factor lies in creating an effective conglomeration between the bye laws of the society, human systems evolution which finds its existence within the natural laws that governs the worldly affairs.

(54).

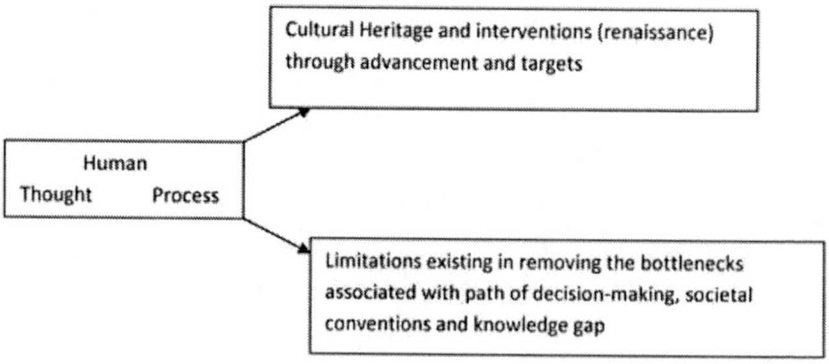
Cultural Heritage and interventions (renaissance) through advancement and targets
Human Thought Process
Limitations existing in removing the bottlenecks associated with path of decision-making, societal conventions and knowledge gap

As the Human Relation School of management states about the securing work performance culture with the purpose of reaching integrated unity which defines its existence in creating bondage in thought process of social dynamics where human instincts acts as a sub system of the natural laws which are the forces of almighty to act as catalyst as stated in Bible (King James version), in part "Isaac at Gerar", where Lord preaches about the act of necessity and divergence resulting in building effective value proposition for restoring the normalcy to Isaac as was in the time of Abraham, the issue of famine. So, discrepancies and action plan with right thought process is very well governed by the natural laws of the world and we human beings as social entities try to develop general tendencies of mapping the issues to particular solutions that at times are dynamic or at times rigid as we can see that Isaac was in a transformation mood regarding finding a right solution as to tackle issues (famine in this case), without analysing the value judgement. Managerial concepts, attitude, cultural disparities, capability building, assessing skills are subject to human thought process and behavioural skills modeling that are brought out through generations and systems evolution as brought out in the Man in the garden of Eden in Bible and the same was echoed by Swami Vivekananda at the World parliament of Chicago as the worldly system is prone to change the capability in management lies in becoming a successful change agent. A change agent's key success factors can include diagnosing the strategies of reality through quantifying the magnitude of system re engineering, designing the basic ground principles on the basis of inter personal relations, conflict management, knowledge sharing, authority delegation, streamlining the divisional strategies with the integrated whole vision as a gain sharing plan, so one's spiritual element as a transformation from sub conscious state of mind to conscious state of mind occurs for balancing growth to maturity through focused differentiation strategies which is an approach towards scientific management. So, we can see how the cause and effect relationship is being formed between the spirituality factor and scientific system to define human interactions which is the essence of management as brought out in Gita in the form of moral paradox, the outcome of which is ethical and value-based leadership.

(55). The gap between development and stagnation of growth lies in adaptability and genuineity of its application.

Management in Real Sense:-

Management being a social concept, its essence lies in how we define our logical framework, create congenial atmosphere to apply knowledge by eradicating disparities existing in our thought process that is what was remarked by Lord Krishna in Gita as to how we define our self existence in link with bye laws of the society, create win-win situation among peers by inter mingling cultural disparities, bridging knowledge gap arising out of generations, analysing communication touch points through baselining the act of transforming approach to practice, value based leadership aligned to crisis management related to balancing the status quo of authority for crisis with adhering to the principles of managing diversity, performing need based analysis to reflect on common concerns, evaluating growth vs. sentiments, and personifying peers issues as self issues for better analysis of the problem solving situations. Thus, 21st century managerial skills are based upon three pillars:-

- Aligning value systems to knowledge sharing in an integrated manner
- Cultivating creativity by leveraging on equal rights to sustainable growth and revenue driven programmes
- An act of gaining social consciousness through aligning the diverging thought process into one logical strategy

Management concept and philosophy counterparts draws its foundation from Gita and Bible, which throws light upon the human system and its evolution vis a vis management dynamics that exists in the form of unity in diversity, preserving cultural heritage in the form of continuity in learning and creativity, balancing power to accountability, connecting minds through team synergy by eliminating negative attitude, deals with the issue as to whether management is a distinctive body or is it an act of reincarnation through human intellect and interaction through social system, determining the baseline of structuring the management system that is whether to adapt complete adhocratic or bureaucratic structure or a balance of it and finally to determine whether in democracy the management limitations are governed by legal implications and ethics or through the boundaries created by the change agents in the economic system.

(56). The key to successful managerial practices lies in creating connectivity through minds and intellects, baselining the general level of task acceptance and leveraging on growth and its perfection.

Chapter – 9

Task Analysis Context to Economic and Foreign Policy

The success story of national bonding and a nation's growth is centred on its economic and foreign policies. Any nation during its phase of growth faces three major challenges that are got to do a lot with government system, bureaucracy and its control over the external factors governing the bi-lateral relationship among nations. These are:

- A nation's political background and the locus of control and accessibility to resources.
- Developmental strategies aligned to systematised growth, establishing linkage patterns with nations categorised under same economic system and the bureaucracy structure.
- Proper designing of the regulatory system and creating a win-win situation by establishing a congenial environment on legal affairs, value system and provisions on foreign policies.

What is Task Analysis?

Task analysis lays down the structure of work flow, elements of the job, balance of EQ (emotional quotient) to do with social intelligence vs. IQ, task frequency, complexities associated with its execution, value proposition and the USPs (unique selling proposition) required to define the scope of the task and the associated

(57). Dealing with corruption lies in what type of mindset people have and the values they are relying on rather than on legal enforcement.

parts to it. A task manager shall perform three different identities of a task namely Expected Role, Perceived Role and the Actual Role.

Expected Role-This stage of the task element has to do with laying down the foundation stone or defining the pre-determined work structure. The government establishes the administrative machinery, configures the portfolios and target maps to be achieved on quarterly, monthly basis. The principles of Democracy states the directive principles which acts as governing norms for the countrymen, the tasks needed to be followed during period of normalcy, emergency provisions and in due consideration of national honour. The expected roles of the government at a glance:-

- Balancing the configuration of the economic system with respect to capitalism and government interventions
- Quantifying the value proposition in terms of the extent of supremacy (onus of control), cost-benefit analysis and tenure of development
- Stabilising the growth in terms of economic barriers, policy maturity phase and creating transformation (renaissance)
- Targeting on bridging the gap on gender in terms of population empowerment and skill substitution
- Designing of the regulatory factors, quota systems and establishing the principles of good governance

Perceived Role-This element decides on the roadmap that the government should adopt to implement its policies and the work agenda. It's a consensus that should be achieved between the government, planning department, other government bodies to bring out the diverse viewpoints under one roof. The challenge is to act as a change agent in terms of mutual benefit gained in bi-lateral agreements with other nations, retention provision, political interests and exploring the unexplored paths on the basis of joint ventures. The perceived role challenges are hurdles existing in educating masses on the role of development, catalytic forces shaping the need terms that focuses on variability existing in economic requirements of the nations, aging economy, impact of constraints of growth of the other nation and policy renewal views.

(58). Need Analysis and desires must align with the limitations imposed by an entity's overall requirement and legacy of achievements.

Actual Role-It is concerned with putting the scenario thinking and action items into result oriented approach. The government action items implementation can be in the form of welfare terms (health, education), resources re-configuration, scheme promotions, entering into new partnerships, community planning and strengthening its position both internally in the form of work relevance and externally in the form of engaging with developmental strategies with other nations of mutual importance. The foreign policy implementation has to do with developmental re organisation, money value promotion, smooth exchange circulation, multi-cultural diversity management, aligning growth tactics, and managing expectations and dependency factors of a nation on another.

Now, it may so happen that a task manager uses either of these or a combination of these, where we have to look into different spheres of outcomes that are achieved as a complete outcome of a task or its partial fulfillment.

Case 1:- (Expected, Perceived Role):

(a) Impact study of policy models on a particular segment of population, zone, area of policy in the form of economic, defence, education, country specific in foreign policy. (In terms of Expected Role).

(b) Constraints imposed by the societal factors, cultural heritages, developmental compositions and external forces in the form of allies, legal issues, and consensus on scope and area unexplored to gain mutual win-win situation. (In terms of Perceived Role).

Case 2:-(Expected, Actual Role):-

(a) The Government may aim on re configuration of its administrative machinery based on the task to be performed at hours of need for national honour. It can be either in the form of fulfilling the basic, safety and augmented needs of the people or to overcome the shortfalls that existed in its previous agenda for development and work schedule. (In terms of Expected Role).

(b) The actual role is in terms of measuring the capabilities that may exist in the form of realising and executing the

(59). Designing the X-factor strategy with sound principles lies in bridging the gap between "what-if analysis" and key issues required for designing the sustainable strategy plan.

dimensions of growth policy, weightage provided and allocated to terms of agreements with respect to project tenures, work proposal aging, understandability between the two governments, economic and social systems prevailing in the nations and tenure of relationship shared. It will also cover within its scope the work flow deviations and the value proposition covering the concerned nation's philosophy of administration – democratic, socialistic which carries a lasting impression on the balancing of power and politics. (In terms of Actual Role).

Case 3:-(Perceived, Actual Role):-

(a) What-if analysis on the part of acting as a change agent in the event of conforming to regulatory guidelines, barriers due to support in terms of financial resources, technology, infrastructure and community planning. (In terms of perceived role).

(b) The actual role in this case will be the specifications laid down to establish smooth transformation process in the form of information management on guidelines, network management in terms of exploring options with a common cause of resource mapping to growth stability and planning on urbanisation for community development. (In terms of Actual Role).

So, in the above cases we can find how an individual or an entity can avail their options to exercise their task structure in an effective manner which involves adherence to planning cycle, generating opportunities and also determining to what extent the task path is matured enough to explore the various dimensions of the work.

The following chart will show us and will give a fair understanding of the diplomatic policy and economic policy evaluations that plays a pivotal in shaping an adequate governance structure.

Case 1: In Terms of Gap Analysis:-

Actual – Perceived Role:-The gap existing in this part can be attributed to the lack of proper defining the planning horizon, setbacks with lasting effect that has been suffered in terms of crisis and

(60). The study of differentiation between X and Y Generation lies in analysing the nature of task variability rather than focusing on limitations that is existing or existed within the time frame of economic renaissance.

negligence, lack of adaptability to external factors both in terms of opportunity and hindrances and lack of flexibility in the administrative wing of the government that makes it too conservative and slow in terms of responsiveness to growth.

Actual – Expected Role:-In this sphere the focus area lies in the area of criteria evaluation done in terms of policy implementation, value proposition scope and preciseness, stability in the political, economic climate and balancing it vis a vis the external relationship, tracking the linkage patterns existing between the economic systems of the nations supporting development of same nature, a nation's past civilisation history, cultural nourishment, re defining the strength of a nation that acts as its competitive advantage which varies in the form of mineral resources, defence, economy, governance structure and human capital.

Case 2: Governance Evaluation Matrix:-

Factors	*Evidence*	*Importance*
Maintain stability in the governance system		
Complexity existing in framing the planning horizons		
Influence tactics used to acquire strategic partnerships		
Balancing Need Analysis to Economic limitations		
Adaptability and adherence to external liabilities and onus of control		

The evaluation sheet that I have presented above is also an indicator to the level of flexibility and defining of the key success factor existing in balancing the level of adhocratic and bureaucratic structure in the administrative machinery and policy making dynamics. As good governance is the call of the day one needs to be vigilant on not only carrying out its capabilities but also undertaking due adherence to principles of governance, analysing the limitations in the systems both as imposed and natural and redefining the value system not only in the form of existing beliefs but also of something that has reason to value as a judgemental factor.

Annexures

Annexure - 1
Learning Attributes Model

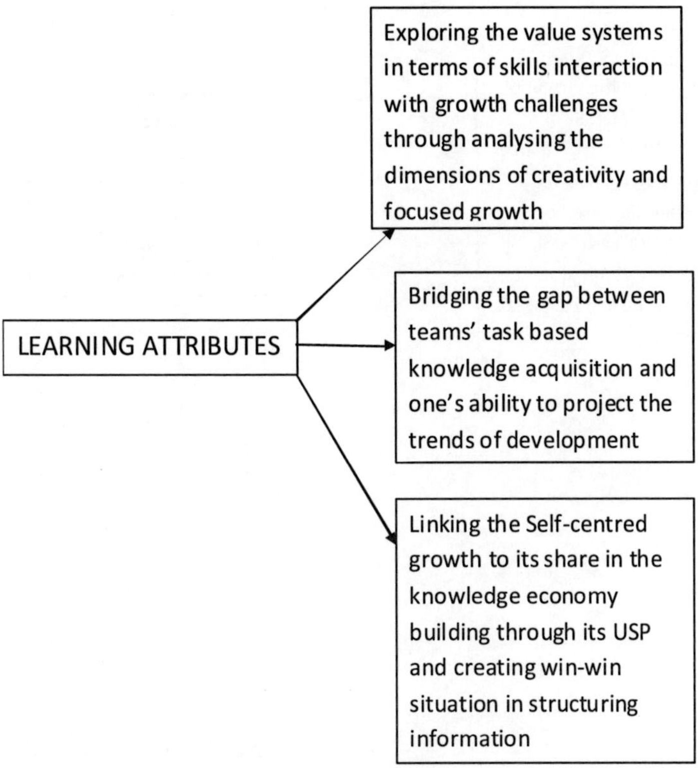

Annexure - 2

Strategies for Survival & Growth

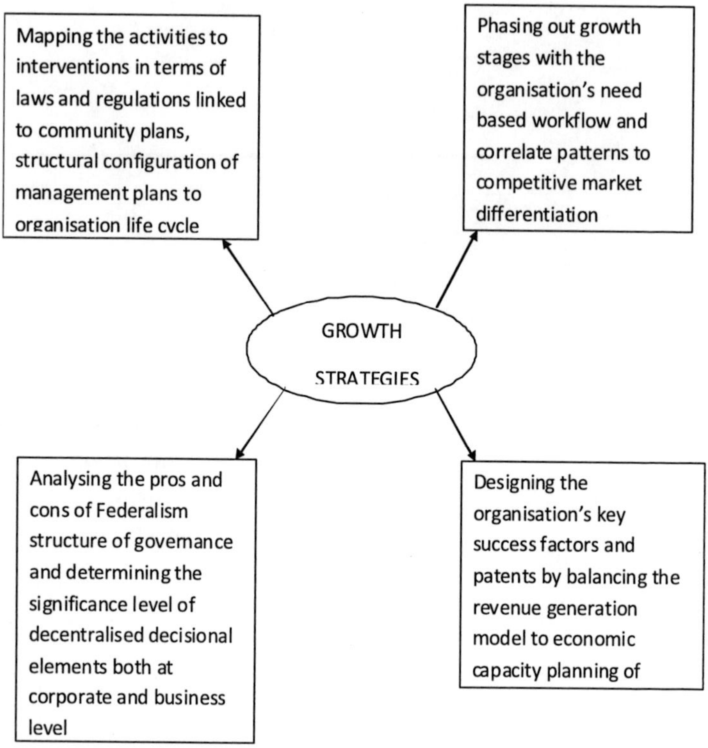

Annexure - 3

Creating Welfare Economy Model

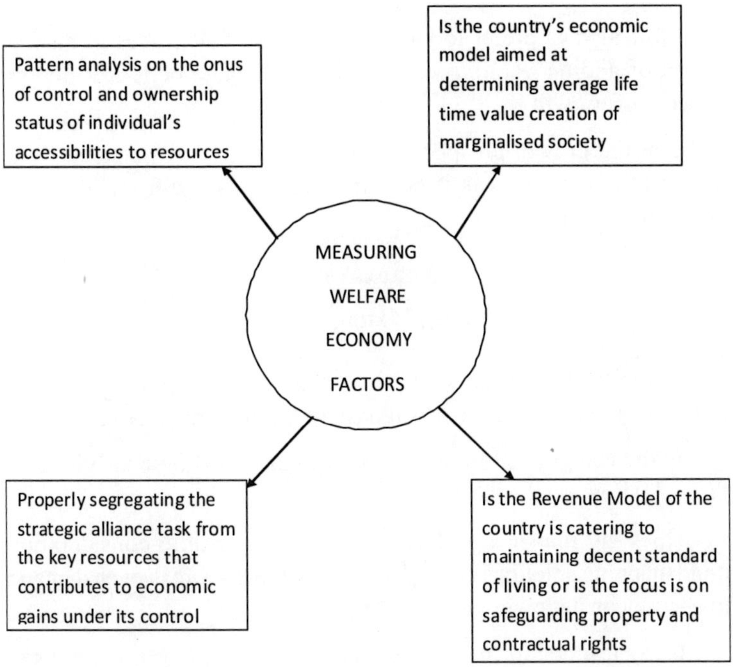

Annexure - 4

Questionnaire on Thinking Analysis

Are my thinking dimensions based on background knowledge or the factual constraints of a situation?

Is the strategic scope of decisional analysis based upon group dynamics value judgement or is it an all times micro managing factor analysis task?

Do I always search for new angle in my decisional process or do I always like to rest upon conservative action plans?

Do my decisions reflect an epitome of self managed tactics or is it the team based thought management process?

What are the bottlenecks that generally exist in the decision making process with reference to cultural conflicts, evaluation of risk appetite in strategising the entity's work flow and analysing the lasting effects?

Do I always prefer to have a framework that comes in distinct forms of adding value to competitive advantage or is it a one go process of growth?

Are the growth prospects for my entity and my personal skills are in alignment and is it contributing to win- win situation for competitive success?

Annexure - 5

Analysing Managerial Tactics

Is the leadership path based on rigid societal conventions and pre-conceived ideologies or is it based on situational analysis?

Is the categorisation of self assessment based on peer views or through situational analysis?

Does my managerial decision making takes into consideration mind mapping solutions centred towards achieving break even demand to ensure constancy in growth?

Is my leadership strategy autonomous in nature or is centralised in nature?

Is my managerial hierarchy based upon influential tactics of leadership or does it involve transparency in decisional process?

Annexure - 6
Strategic Maps vs. Growth Mobility

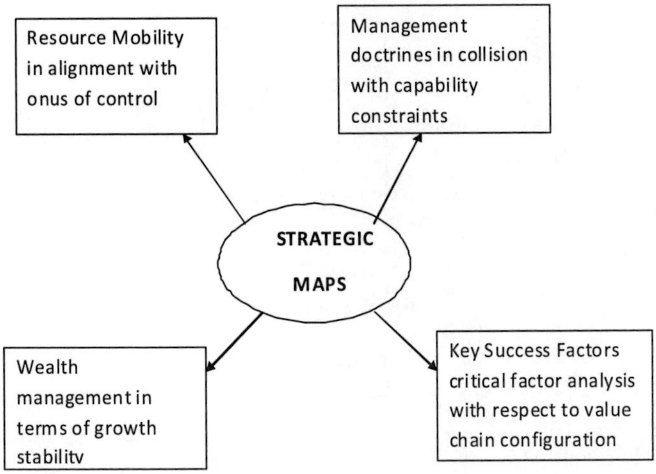

Annexure - 7
Leadership Traits and Motivation

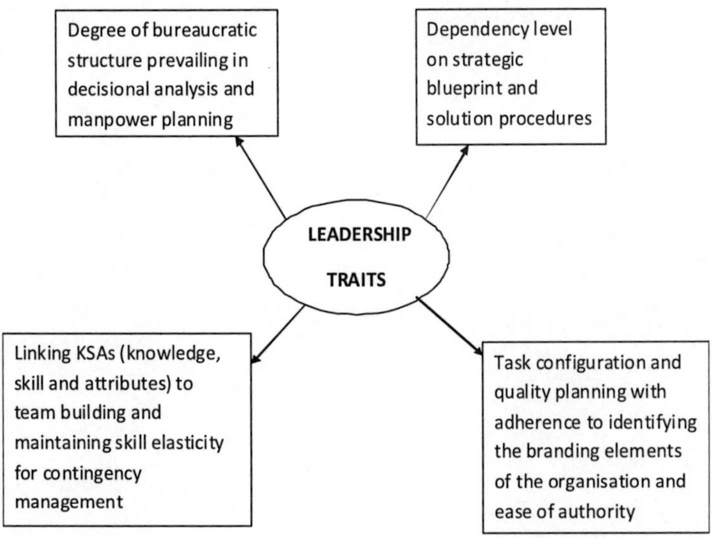

Annexure - 8
Creativity and Innovation

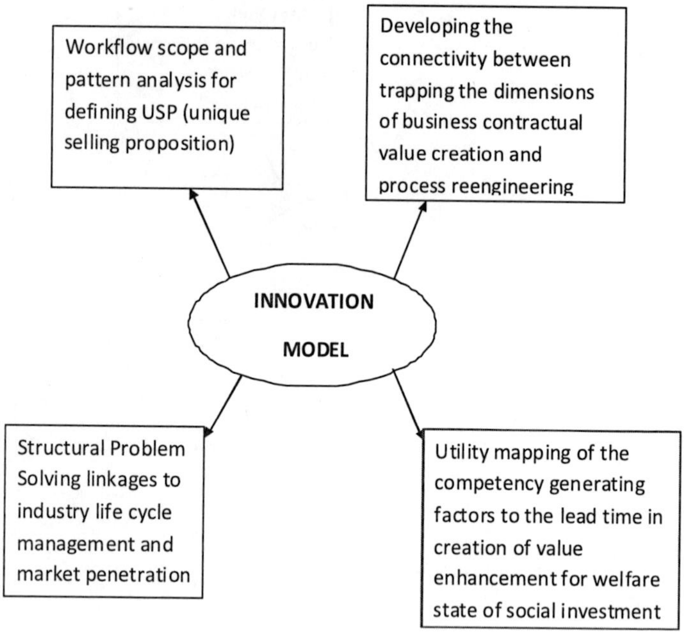